There once lived a man called Nehemiah.
He lived in the town of Susa.

His job was to taste wine for the king.

One day Nehemiah heard some news that made him very sad.

He had heard that the walls in the famous city of Jerusalem had been broken down.

Nehemiah prayed to God about the situation.

The king saw that Nehemiah was sad and asked him what was wrong.

Nehemiah told the king all about the walls. The king told Nehemiah to return and help rebuild them.

The King told Nehemiah to take wood with him.
Soon banging and tapping could be heard as the
work began.

However, there were some bad men around, Sanballat and Tobiah, who laughed at those who were working.

Nehemiah had guards placed
along the walls to protect the
workers.

There was so much work to do that the workers had to
spread out along the walls.

Nehemiah told the people to remember that God was with them.

In 52 days the walls were finished.

Nehemiah called people to be leaders
People were chosen to live in the city.

One day, Ezra the prophet stood in the city and read the law of Moses to all the people.

It was time for a celebration to remember that God was their strength.

This story can be found in the Bible in the book of Nehemiah.